The Great Wave

The Great Wave

RON SLATE

Houghton Mifflin Harcourt

BOSTON   NEW YORK   2009

For information about permission to reproduce selections
from this book, write to Permissions, Houghton Mifflin
Harcourt Publishing Company, 215 Park Avenue South,
New York, New York 10003.

www.hmhbooks.com

Library of Congress Cataloging-in-Publication Data
Slate, Ron.
  The great wave / Ron Slate.
    p. cm.
  ISBN 978-0-547-23274-4
  I. Title.
  PS3619.L365G73 2009
  811'.6—dc22   2008037385

Book design by Melissa Lotfy
Text is set in Aldus

Printed in the United States of America

MP 10 9 8 7 6 5 4 3 2 1

for Nancy

and for all who remember
Carey and Charles Tenen

Contents

II

The feeling that if the slightest crack opened up in this enclosed vision, all things could spill out beyond the four points of the horizon, leaving you naked and alone, begging alms, muttering imprecise words, without this amazing preciseness you had seen.

—George Seferis, journal, October 21, 1946

To the One Who Hears Me

In the fifth year of friendship
he asked permission to tell his secret,
suggesting we go to a donut shop nearby.
Grand theft, drug dealing, a year on Rikers Island.

Now I have hustled you to this other spot
without even a cup of coffee to offer
nor for that matter to take you
into my confidence.

The great felons exceed the petty thieves
in intuition, the greatness unmeasured
by the size or value of what is removed,
but rather in the shuffle and the shift.

The shock was not in the details,
the carjacking of a famous quarterback's convertible,
"actually his wife's," but my realizing
he recognized the level of my listening.

This intimacy—all to help him appear to grasp
the vexing source of manic energy
agitating everyone on the job.
In the telling, he in his suit became a white man

selling crack out of a red Saab
with the top down three blocks north
of MLK Boulevard. His former roommate, the quarterback,
helped spring him early with a personal appeal.

He was saying: Make use of me,
all my skills are now at your disposal,
trust my boldness, and when you discover the way
into your fortune, take me with you.

We sat in the shadow of our office tower
and he knew whom he was talking to.
Just as I am speaking to you now,
not exactly waiting for your reply.

I

Meditation by the Sea

Engines, the slitting hiss of tires on asphalt,
doors opening and slamming, footsteps on stone,
then on carpeting. Keystrokes, devices beeping.

For years these bland sounds saved me.
Welcome, they said, to our confines.

But don't think the times were uneventful.
In fact, they seemed supernal,
as when people first figured out the gods
caused the world to cohere but could perform
nothing miraculous. The coherence amazed.

Other sounds then—at the beach, my children
invented names for the rocks in the surf.
America was closest to shore, then Haystack.
Farthest out, Neptune, often invisible.

Sometimes my ear would catch the cry
of a mud swallow, or the motor of a plane
tugging a sign, or the puncture of a beer can.
But it was as if these sounds were enclosed
elsewhere, like the ear ringing, heard then forgotten.
My daughters' mouths moved soundlessly, on Haystack.

Did I begin too receptive to the world's sounds,
needing closure—or sealed from the messages,
in need of piercing? Should I try to hear
above the roar, or speak to it,
or against it?

Watch This Space

Whatever appears wants to attach emotionally.

Nothing appears.

All that might be but is not.

When there's no demand, all eyes come to me—
there's room for everyone.

A voice resistant to its own proposals.

And a row of pigeons facing sunset.

My beloved exists in a backward time.
Which of us is the screen the night air flows through
as we lie there not speaking?

Still an excess.

So much work to make it useful.

I've said nothing—and already, my late period.

But deep in this white space is the real thing.

Come to me, I'm yours, since you regard me
with such pure blank love.

At the Swedish Embassy

A mature linden in bloom,
humid June evening in D.C.
Swedish entrepreneurs came closer
to say their names on the terrace,
among peonies, spent irises,
and dahlias making their move.

Platters of gravlax and herring,
the air abuzz with "verbal agreements"—
together we will engineer impatiens
able to survive a hard frost,
now that the steep helix of the northern hemisphere
has been scaled, the code manifest,
their vodka on our ice.

The Swedes say the world started like this:
an abyss, to the north a cold world,
to the south a kingdom of torches.
Frosty mist rose from a frigid well,
a frozen stream to fill the void,
then southern flares fell into the ice,
and droplets changed into beings.

Runic script on the rusted leaves
of the hollyhock. A napkin on the lawn.
The ambassador's wife confided:

"I would much rather talk
with one person. Do you know
the poetry of Tranströmer?
Every person is a half-open door
leading to a room for everyone.
Apparently that room is in my house,
since we endlessly entertain."

But absent of us, her garden
would have merely drifted into dusk,
no longer pleasing and admired.
We stood there in that simple darkness.

Was this why I sensed the brief lives
of bedding plants as if for the first time?
No, because it was *the first time.*

Must my approach be so clever, so facile?
Answer that one yourself.

In the dimmest light, the linden's scent
turned oppressive. It was time to design
a way to outlive all urgencies.
Thus I conceived a brilliant marigold
to last an eternal age of ice.

Ici Mort Robert Desnos

In the anthology of elegies, every voice moans:
I am not yet a dark shape, my mourning
is not maudlin, and I feel the full weight
of the casket and its content of memory.

When the bus arrived at the Little Fortress,
there were yellow streaks in the air.
A cold noon in April, the dim voice
of a German tour guide spoke of Robert Desnos,
who was one of those sallow flashes.

My wife found the plaque marking his death,
in the barracks, and came to find me
alone on the bus dreaming in a viral fever—
my dead cousin Charles and I
planning our trip to La Creuse,
the town Sardent and the village Villevégoux,
where our family waited for the war
to recede to the Rhine, the road clear to Paris.
But now I'll never see those places.

They're trying to live again at Terezín,
a bakery, a grocery among shadows.
A cautious girl running home
with bread. When my wife found me,
she looked as if we'd been deprived
of all those years together.

Now I'll never go to La Creuse,
tracing the escape from Paris,
Charles and I laughing at folly in a rented Renault.
When my grandfather found him and my uncle Marcel
with their bathtub overflowing in a hotel
above the rooms of the German command,
he slapped them for stupidity.

They say Desnos read the jaundiced palms
of fellow detainees and found good fortune.
This is the air we inherit, moist with delirium,
the faintest smell of something baked.

The dead ones say: Never-to-Return,
you are a dark shape
among flaring arcs, your grieving matters less
than an eyelash of the woman you dream of so much,
and a desperate love drifts down on you
like ashes in a forecast of sunlight.

Cocoanut Grove

My life began with the fire,
glimmering in the birthwaters.
Beyond my bedroom wall
voices murmured a memory.

My father's mother died
with her sister in the ladies' room.
He said—if she had escaped to Shawmut Street,
been saved, nothing would be the way it is.
How is it? drifted over my route to school.

I stared at a wire service photo
fixed with brutal light, a fire hose
snaking through soaked debris,
faces slack with shock, bodies
laid out on the sidewalk.

How compelling for a family
to have such a story to relate.
Nothing would be the way it is.
To speak of a desirable world,
the listening boy leaning in.

November in Boston, women
collapsed waiting for their coats,
the ceiling's satinette billows

crackled and melted and were drawn
into their throats. A shoe
wedged in the revolving door.

A face pressed against glass.
The fireball—bright orange,
or bluish with a yellow cast,
or a blistering white.

The nightclub burned in minutes,
in 1942, with a sibilant exhalation.
My grandfather, sworn in, testified,
but a single night evades judgment,
bloated with unassignable blame.

Corrosive worm of remembrance,
allure of the lurid past,
the nozzle's snout regressing
down the smoldering street.
Adoring the damaged world,
we abused it, we refused
to let the sea wind clear the smoke.

So now it's time to decide how to move
within spaces on the sites of catastrophe,
how to regard the atria and the lobbies,

even as the alarms sound,
evacuations rehearsed, the streets
filling with imaginary survivors,

just as the boy, surviving boyhood,
said *So that's how it is,* just before
sleep settled on him like asbestos.

Questionnaire to the Dead

(regarding repatriation by the Conciliation Commission)

1
Do you prefer to return
to what is now our world, whether or not
you could inhabit your former home?

2
If you prefer *not* to return,
indicate in order of preference
other worlds where you would like to live.

3
If your preference is to return, would you agree
to live at peace with the living
as a law-abiding resident of our world?

Khrushchev's Foot

Looming before us is the pale, tender,
childlike foot of Nikita Khrushchev.
Size 7 or 8, "like a boy's" according
to Sergei, his son, on the lecture circuit.

A shoe meant a lot to a Russian foot,
something you'd tug off a frozen corpse.
A shoe meant a lot to a British head of state,
to tap a shoe on the rostrum in Parliament
expressed the highest degree of obstruction.

So when Khrushchev slammed his shoe on a desk
in the U.N., it meant megatons to us
but just a parliamentary flourish to him,
designed to make P.M. Macmillan, orating
unmemorably, feel at home.

Such a delicate foot, veined and moist —
it makes me want to reveal a secret,
an expendable one, declassified.

One night when I was seven years old,
my father woke me at three A.M.
to scan the sky for the coming
of the satellite, Khrushchev's star.
There was nothing to impede the view,

not a wisp of cloud. So small and sharp,
bristling with speed, and gone —

it was then I knew I wanted to be
something to admire. Maybe to fear.
Of course, the massing of mistrust
between father and son,
our standoff in the Divided City,
had something to do with it.

Disclosed: the Premier told his aides
to place a shoe under his desk.
A single American penny loafer.
Agrarian reformer on a hot day in May,
he had walked into the General Assembly
wearing socks and sandals.

If a person's nature is harsh
and resolute, may it also keep us
vigilant and entertained.
Years later, the child may explain
exactly what the father meant to say.

Dinner for My Fifty-sixth Birthday

Mêng Chiao asked:
"What troubling wave can arrive to vex
a spirit like water in a timeless well?"

Or so these lines were quoted over *primi piatti,*
followed by comment and riposte as the cork
burst out with a shout of relief.

You have such aplomb, she said to me,
I bet if a bomb blew up in the street
you wouldn't even flinch.

We could clearly see the water
in our glasses was never entirely still,
having flowed so long to pause there.

Anchored on the River Ch'u,
Mêng Chiao saw marshland swollen with moonlight.
Some must believe he was tranquil,

transcending a time of bivouacked armies
on opposing shores. Others say his question
was a vision of approaching disaster,

and that transcendence is for selfish losers.
Wreckage of mussel and clam shells—
fondness alone can't suffice,

since I seek out my friends, but with dessert
comes the urge to preserve the source
of affection, to stare down the well,

wonder at the rumble in the earth,
lie alone at anchor, and accommodate
the mechanism of catastrophe.

Morbidezza

I was proud of my prudence —
when the goddess emerges, gazing
straight ahead while descending the stone steps,
you don't reach out to touch her.

In my studio, sketching with ink,
I studied her flesh solemnly,
toiling like a cartographer's apprentice,
tracing rivers, ranges, and borders.

My pregnant wife didn't care
for such imagery, she suspected
this absorption in absent powers,
a dispassionate alertness

for some fascinating presence.
I rose from my chair, left my desk,
and abandoned the art for twenty years.
I took a job, traveled often, rarely alone.

Returning, I discovered a daughter,
then another, then again.
Sometimes, gashes and cuts, weeping —
I would clean their wounds.

Sometimes I touched the hands,
the backs of knees, shoulder blades.
Then a car drove me to the airport.
When I returned they kissed me noisily.

Their senses tracking me precisely,
they smelled my hair, they could not stop
touching me. Something familiar in this,
the coy eyes pleading and at times

deceitful, the bodies emerging.
Unlike the résumé, the soul is structured
without a scheme or reason —
so the body compels conclusions.

Where once I saw my wife's body
standing between me and a specter,
I now stood pitched between my wife
and the suntanned backs of my departing daughters.

Our house billows with their absent scents.
What's left me now is the old art.
My wife smiles to see me try my hand
at arousing an aging goddess

and writing down the song she sings —
Our flesh is here for you,
a world is here for you,
only for you, just beyond your reach.

The Garden of Flowing Fragrance

Since it was disrespectful to address the teacher
by his given name, he suggested *Call me something generic,*
and then announced what he had in mind,
a one-word name revered even today,

                                 because there's no harmony
under heaven unless we accomplish the naming.

Dynasties later, during the Age of Division,
when a man (salt merchant, silk merchant) gained wealth enough
to afford the keep of his own walled-in garden, names of plants drifted out
from the flowering paths of the government palaces.
He would sit on a stone bench among the blossoms,
saying their names and smoking his pipe.
Then, the names of his parents, wife and children,
then his city and its streets, the professions, the sports,
the many pleasures and the kinds of poverty,
all manner of food and things in the marketplace,
and on and on, you can imagine.

He thought, *Am I the only person who can see
there is only one world?* You sit alone long enough,
the heart calms down yet beats faster.
But maybe that's the tobacco.

Now here we are in The Pavilion of a Thousand Poets,
gazing across the pond fringed by oaks and tall pines.

There's a story — Louis asked George, *Whose poetry do you prefer,*
mine or yours? George replied *Mine*
and that was the end of the friendship.

You and I, here in California, our bags and laptops
in the trunk of the rental car. It's all right that you don't read poetry,
since you're lovely — just as the sponsors of this classic garden
make exceptions for us, since the symbology
carved by crews of Chinese stonemasons working eight hundred tons
of many-hued sculptural limestone mined from Lake Tai
escapes us.

        Rejecting "The Garden That Invites the Ocean"
as well as "The Garden of Awakening [flower to be named],"
the committee selected "The Garden of Flowing Fragrance,"
though the vote wasn't unanimous — perhaps the reason
the scent of peach, plum, jasmine, and sweet olive
seems indelicate, blossom petals blowing around.
Once a thing is named, the process is inexorable.

Carved into the wood panels of the pavilion,
into the paving stones, the tiles . . .

That moment, when one says *wind*
instead of *breeze.*

Under the Pergola

An Adirondack chair, painted in a primary color,
in one corner, under the pergola, the blooming vine
appealing above — people an abundance
of themselves, prodigal in sunglasses, in the shade.

Will I speak to him, and if so, do I call him
"Mr. Secretary"? He groans into his chair,
opens the *Times*, reads, then glances at me,
and I stare over the edge of my Asian novel.

Many years after the war he speed-walked
through the streets of Hanoi in his jogging suit,
then around the Lake of the Restored Sword.
Nine years ago, but now he struggles with his cane.

Between what I can see, wedged in this chair,
and the explanations of what I'm seeing,
there is a chasm. As between the ink on his fingers
and the pronouncements quoted on the page.

Anything to fill that desolate space.
This is why we follow a man who describes
what seems to be occurring in the plosive world,
who paints the face of evil on a three-minute egg.

The old man's wife sits in the third chair,
the nurse dozes in the fourth corner. "Bobby,
come sit *here,* in the shade," and so he lifts
himself up painfully, shuffles across, and sags

with a wailing sound. Nine years ago,
before meeting with his former enemies,
he walked around the Lake of the Restored Sword—
where the fisherman Le Loi long ago found

a magical sword in his net, swung it three times
above his head, and led his people to throw
the Chinese out of Vietnam. When he returned
to thank the spirit of the lake, a giant tortoise

made off with the sword. The Emperor Le Loi
stared into the depths of the lake, two passive eyes
returned his gaze, during the liquid hour of peace
and the weeks of warm memories of war.

December the First, Terminal A

When I dropped off my parents,
curbside with state troopers hastening our farewells,
it was like delivering them to the afterlife.
They vanished even as I turned away.

The two of them on board, no hunger, no meal,
their memories flaring and fading. Meds in the carry-on.

One night I drove to their house—they were excited,
having just watched, live on an all-news network,
a jet ditch at LAX with no landing gear.
Driving home, I heard on the radio—
passengers witnessed their own approach, skid
and salvation, as in-flight entertainment.

One morning my first thought was—
a man waking is a man wanting something.
Soon after, I canceled a trip to a country
I'd always wished to see.
All things in us occur at once.

Anita O'Day died at eighty-six, two days before
December the first, my parents flying
to Florida, spotless belongings shipped ahead.
There my father will turn eighty-five, tracking
my mother's sugar count, listening to Anita O'Day,

who never cared if we never knew her,
and made us feel unknown.

My oldest daughter, neuro-oncology nurse,
on my cellphone as I left Logan,
said she'd attended her first patient death.
She wept with the family, cutting life support.
The last breath was an inhalation.

The terror of airports is not my terror,
which is more modest, fear of lingering,
of failing to turn away. Like a blood oath
between brothers, my soul and I sing a song
to each other, such as "My Old Flame,"
ardently flubbing the lyrics.

When I die my daughters may say *He hath ever*
but slenderly known himself—yet rushed, I'm able
gladly to part and drive away,
mindful of the urgencies of the law,
ignorant not of my love but its length.

Impromptu

Don't call out to the world,
since it can't answer in one voice.
You're ill equipped to evaluate
such a havoc of response.
If you've been passed from woman to woman
like a celebrity tabloid at the beach,
be satisfied you learned to stay
crisp and dry. The women amuse themselves
with anecdotes about you,
losing truth with each telling.
They've taught you to get dressed,
present yourself to a world
you can't enter. So the world approaches
while you stare at the sea,
an enclosure instead of an entrance.
Look behind you — the hills, the city.
But don't long for pine-scented shade,
or the discreet frisk of the security guard,
or the obsessive psyche of the ocean —
but a blending of uncertain potential.
The peril of the mackerel, closing in
on prey near the shore, is that he's trapped
between the sea bass and the sand.
Adore the voices, not the stories of yourself.
To the one who asks *What are you thinking*

when you gaze at the water?—
answer, as the mackerel die en masse,
I was thinking of you.

after Mêng Chiao

Lion of God

Some remember me from those days,
not by that name, given to me,
but by the breach between name and boy.

At ten I pronounced the unspeakable
name of God, my teacher rose from his chair,
dragged me by the scruff, then shook me

in his teeth. Speaking the word to make
a pleasing sound, I neglected
to consider the significance,

committing a grave offense.
Thus I was transformed by terror,
my classmates looking on,

and in the space between name and child
arose fear, respect, contempt,
wonder, loss of faith, awe of the eternal.

I took my seat and read on, wary
of meaning but loving the lilt, relying now on rhythm
so that time may never be interrupted again.

Strophe

Far out on an island in the harbor,
recruits rehearsed in burning rooms.
We could see the training tower flaming
like a floating candle, even at noon.

There are other islands, some barren,
some with remains of old use.
Of course, the burning spectacle drew
my attention, apt to dissolve
in the sea, lulled by the sound
of waves both imperative and dull.

Pessoa wrote: Even if you sail
across every sea, all you learn
is the breadth of your own boredom.
Without the plume of smoke,
the ocean blurs to abstraction.

For years my colleagues believed
I was thoughtful when silent, figuring the angles,
cracking the shell of a new idea,
but it was as if waves, droning intimately,
murmured in my ear, *senseless.*

When a fireman dies on the job,
usually the heart fails. So they practice technique
in a simulated six-story elevator shaft.
All around them, but unable to distract,
a tide surges below their six-hour session
of discipline and skill, and a nimbus
of fuming haze hovers above the tower.

After so many years, has something been saved for me?
Although I don't know what to make
from a flicker on the water, I fear
what would happen if that flame,
so precisely seen, were to subside.

While we ate our lunch on the seawall,
talking of our times, unprepared to interpret,
distracted by what we noticed,
something ignited for fighters to withstand
and recruits rappelled with deadweight dummies.

Foghorn, Daybreak

The day began with forgetting.
I had fallen asleep in a darkness
I could see into, I woke in withholding light.
This happened in a hotel room
one block up from the pier.
The harbor and the street were silent.

The foghorn did its work quickly.
The first sound was purposeful,

then a sinking note took hold.
In my time, which is a repeating phrase,
I learned not to blame the foghorn
for the dangers it calls to mind.

But one must never forgive
the foghorn for exploiting
an eagerness to respond to any call.

The mordant remark of a woman
may reach the shore as a two-toned utterance
from the unloved life of the ocean.

At a late hour I had opened my eyes
to the flickering screen—
Chet Baker was running out of the surf

at Malibu, glistening and dissolute.
The ocean wanted him drowned.
His audience wanted some response,
but he was aloof to all but the music.
In his tone, sensitive.
In his expression, lost.

In my hotel room, at daybreak,
the blinds were vaguely lit.
What then seeped in, what lay upon me?
I had dreamed of my mother, collapsed
on the lawn at a wedding, staring up
uncomprehending, in a diabetic swoon.

The first sound was *You hear*
my voice, don't you?
The second was *Imagine me beside you*
in the deep, pulling you down.

II

The Great Wave

I predict, like the one who was sucked to sea
and returned in an Arabian container ship,
all small worlds will be dashed and drowned.

I witnessed this deliverance on a silent television,
my fingers disquieted a bowl of almonds,
a librarian called to say Constantinople is on hold.

The entire surface trembled, an oscillation
like a bell. When the seismologist said the Eurasian plate
"delivered a blow to our planet," his words

were almost enough to renew our belief
in the earth's roundness, the tidal sugars and salts
of our bodies, the atonement of death squads.

When I was a child, I discovered my depravity
among the other boys — but we were sanguine all the same,
with the fortitude to face what we'd found.

So now, led to abandon the world
for word of the world's moments,
one must be cautious and deliberate.

I had a dream — high-water marks on the side
of my house, the aftermath of a deluge
rising from a spring in the cellar.

I didn't realize the floodwaters would recede
with the violence of their rising, fishing boats
torn from moorings, dome of the mosque collapsed.

You who savor the scent of the linden
live in a small world, and I also speak
from cramped provisional space.

On the stacked ship they videotaped
as they passed, then circled back to pluck
a single man from floating debris —

I witnessed this alone on a glowing screen,
I couldn't lift an almond to my mouth,
I was a fallow field ruined by brackish flood,

but I would choose the wave over the wind,
I would swamp your world with wreckage,
I would hold fast to you, and you would be saved.

The Meeting in Madrid

Listen, the band still plays in the plaza
but my Spanish friends are weary.
They turn from each other sluggishly,
simply tired, but it feels like a misfortune.

Among all people they suffer the most
from prosperity, assuming the habits
of updated Danes, globalized Poles.
Alejandro departs early from his house
in the new suburb, too far to return
for a nap at siesta time, *siete*,
the seventh hour after dawn.

It was my job to incite the nations
to productivity, inducing Greeks to adopt
the advances of Swedes. One could deceive
a whole world by staying alert.

Alejandro's eyelids quivered while the Germans
presented their plan for expansion.
The Spaniards nap in buses,
barber chairs, dressing rooms, toilet stalls.
The most exhausted people of Europe,
deprived of their devoted shadow, their dream.
Caffeinated but dull, fatigued by enthusiasm.

Waking at dawn in New York in 1930,
Lorca lamented the pillars of slime.
He gazed at the palisades and saw,
staggering in the suburbs, insomniacs.

In Madrid I heard the dual tongues
of the present—the first, quelling the tension
felt in the past and feared for the future—
the other, tragic and personal, continuous
with the past, ambiguous, conflicted.
It all made me miss the comfort of my wife.

The hotel manager entered our meeting room
without knocking: a threat,
please take your coats,
there's a breeze this evening,
the police have arrived,
please use the stairway, not the lift.

We waited on the plaza
while the band wondered what to play
at a time like this—something
to console or wake the world,
or simply to please themselves.

Samba de Orfeo

Before I could react — three men, and she was gone.

Could I react? You could say
they succeeded where I failed.

I ran after the van, a few blocks — I'm not so young anymore.

In São Paolo, one becomes accustomed
to the kidnappings, the reasonable ransoms.

Criminals and corrupt policemen, in league.

Today — my car doors reinforced, the glass
double-thick, my route guided by satellite.

Her family paid for long-term protection.

She returned in good health, feeling desirable,
needing no escort and now fearing no captor.

My fear for her — the market for body parts.

She'd go on and on about migraines,
I'd be transfixed by her earlobe.

One's love is really no concern of the beloved.

I rise from my chair in the *churrascaria,*
between meat courses, and dance around the salads.

Even if one is loved in return.

Waxing Gibbous

The answering world took the form
of a new country. The question was—
will we continue to be hunted?

This is your moon, this is your sea,
said my grandfather, lighting a Chesterfield.
We were sitting on the wall at Wollaston Beach.

My grandmother recalled—the youngest
of the soldiers began to weep.
Her soup reminded him of something.

Five of them, searching for weapons.
When they left, she kept the food warm
for the underground, hiding below the farm.

So as a boy I could not avoid seeing
my mother as a girl, in her bed, straining
for the sound of engines, her boots ready—

my mother sullen or giddy, singing or stricken,
when I returned from grade school for lunch,
and later, in her bed calling my grandparents

to save her. I played records in my bedroom.
Here is my grandfather's voice quoting Hikmet
in Turkish, then again, "You must grieve for this

right now, you have to feel this sorrow now."
Suddenly she stopped weeping, she spooned
the soup on a tray, and I lifted the needle from the song.

He lit another cigarette, a man was surfcasting,
there was a gibbous moon in the warming sky,
and then a yellow corona in the eye of a bass.

My accumulating moon, the shape
on the morning of my birth,
very nearly full, rising

when few are watching, unnoticed
until the hood of sunset, at times
easily mistaken for something complete.

In the Free Zone

Beside the river you can say anything
you want, the waters protect you from danger.
To comprehend, others must come very close.
But singing is risky, certain melodies
are unmistakable in their intentions.
Even so, it's worse in other places.
Here at least the river runs full, and my friends
laugh at me — "no one wants to listen to *you*."

Sometimes when someone I knew in the city
passes through, he stays at my place for a week —
fried bass and crude beer in unmatched bottles.

One guest — his theme was "I'm experienced."
He'd say, "You get an idea of the girth
of the world, you see yourself in the faces."
But I was contentious, I could see only
one thing in anyone's face and it was fear —

you make it to the free zone, maybe invest
in a small farmhouse, hill up your potatoes
in your muddy sneakers, show them your papers
when they ask for them — they, too, are petrified,
so to keep things amicable, you trade tales
about the fish taken from the river.

The ocean's not far off, you can smell low tide.
Since I don't go far, my friends have given up
inviting me to the beach. At liberty,
I cast my line into the current.

You strive to merge with the face of another,
pretty soon you want his power, his kingdom.
But to act — it's true I've done very little —
there's no achievement, just the arc of an aim
scrambling one's image on the water.

The Gold Rush

Contained in the past is everything withheld,
unearned or deserved, beyond debate.

Not that I walk these streets, but lose balance—
my father, also unsteady, must have wondered why.

The faded glory of the god-as-bull,
the former felicities of the human—

the first gets payback for his past success,
the other for his legendary losses.

The reason is withheld. What metastasized
in the silence of our parents will never be told.

So it seems we speak from a place
not so easy to regard as a *location*.

Yet here are three deer in a suburban yard, displaced,
and an immigrant worker eating his lunch in the shade.

As I age and lose my definition,
any voice could be my own, any scrawl my signature.

All that gold embedded in faces of rock
just off the shoulder of the interstate highway—

a spreading stain of iron oxide tells us it's there,
one-fifth of an ounce per ton of rock,

but no affordable way to mine it. So of course,
what choice do we have but to drive by.

Four Roses

So quiet and undeveloped, the sadness in the father,
like wet porcelain clay in a closet, organic and inert.
He drives to work in the Dodge with the back seat removed
to transport cases of liquor and wine
between his two stores,
                              and the day will be profitable,
the shelves depleted here and there, then restocked,
the ashtrays emptied and the floor mopped.

This is my father and I'm driving my mother's Chrysler
up Quarry Street, a patrol car pulling up behind. Siren.
The cop looks at my license and decides
on a penalty almost biblical in its severity:
he escorts me to my father's store
                              and turns me in,
I figured you'd want to handle this one yourself.

Forty years later, my father and I laugh — laws and violations,
shame and scam, no ticket to pay so maybe you give the cop
something on top of his usual take. Follow the money
and understand how the kickback system works
between distributors and stores.

                              But back to the sadness.
Perhaps "undeveloped" isn't quite right.
Unlike a bartender, a man selling liquor isn't compelled to console

his clientele. Yet each time he sees the stumpy fingers
of a longshoreman when the palm opens for change,
he feels, quite simply, a sadness.

His mother suffocated by smoke,
his fellow airmen spiraling into the bombed Balkans, his wife
shrieking in her sleep.

The tending of a short stack of hundreds.
The son so unachieved, and of no help. His assistant manager,
caught skimming the till, had been stealing for years.
I remember—we were in the yard, I was waiting for him
to answer my question *Is it true?* He kept watering
the one rose bush with the sparse blossoms,
adjusting the nozzle to a finer spray.

Beginning with a Line by Madeleine des Roches

Would you know, traveler, what I used to be?
A young man speaking, harder and harder
to hear. Vanishing into the world's will.
But like you I wanted to persist
with a body and a voice making a case
for the body's service.
I exceeded all expectations in that regard.
People believed I was a bridge,
a cambered arch aspiring in two directions
over black waters. I could go west to the proven,
I could go east to the not-yet-invented.
But I was a man, not a bridge,
leaning on the rail and looking down
at the dredging for the missing person.
A body may condense to its proper shape,
but too late in time to keep its tone,
while the voice negotiates on its own
for a bodily place in an actual world.

Arcadia

A horn blaring and the gut-smash of metal —

I heard the crash and swiveled
on my stool in the Arcadia.

Two drivers met in the street,
chastened and faultless.

Pieces of chrome and glass —

so much care taken not to step
in the spreading puddle of antifreeze.

As children we played in the parking lot
of the hospital, hearing the siren
long before an ambulance arrived.

A policeman said, "You kids go home."

As teens we worked as orderlies,
suddenly we could be trusted to look,
but I soon preferred to avert my eyes.

Notorious intersection,
too costly to redesign.

The insipid righteousness of pedestrians.

Cited, a shaken man,
protesting his innocence —

he took the stool beside me, awaiting the tow,

beneath the bleached print of the Parthenon
and a giant gyro hovering above it
poised to punish or nourish Athens.

You're my witness, he said,
you saw what happened.

But I didn't see anything,
I heard the sound of what occurred,
and then I turned to look.

The Tunnel

Ask me to tell you about my tour,
I'll say I don't remember much.

Name a time, thirty years ago or more,
when you had just come to terms with the world,
and now tell me what you recall of it.

When I returned, I became a person
who can't or doesn't want to tell you anything.
You see so much, it quiets you down.
Of course, there are episodes and facts.
My father talked of bombing Ploesti,
and my children know I drove a truck.

One time, a sniper popped up in our perimeter,
snapped off some rounds into the latrine.
I was unloading frozen steaks for stand-down
while an albino lieutenant, fresh from school,
was calling orders to no one in particular,
violating procedure — *Get down that hole!*

I can see the expression on his face,
the look of an apostle, prestige but no power.
In that year, moving materiel in the heat,
I came to terms with the world.
He was shouting *Now, now, now!*

From this I learned a trade secret:
never count on a single word.

Then there was a thump in the ground.
In the tunnel, the shooter had tripped
his own mine. But when the body was retrieved,
it was a woman. They brought the dogs
to learn the scent of what would kill us.

Aquinas observed that when serfs worked
overtime they'd filch a goose from the flock,
taking no more than what was owed.
A chaplain who'd bum rides to Danang
told me that story, and then he blessed my truck.

The dead woman's body — they heaved it
onto a flatbed, black pajamas in smoking shreds.
You see so much, maybe someone owes you,
but who? Through the shooting and the shouting,
best to mind your own best interests
out the back of your deuce and a half.

Blizzard

The snowdrift is a monument
to the storm passed to sea.
Sunlight piercing at noon —
I avert my eyes from the illumination.
Twenty years ago, just a few miles from here,
my car was stranded in snow.
I'd penciled some words on the back
of a shopping list, *I could actually die out here.*
Furniture was plunging in the surf,
the windshield went blank.
Then the samaritans arrived, struggling hip-deep
behind sweeping beams, coffee on their breath.
Something blowing through and covering the world,
godly or bestial — I had no preference,
lost in the blizzard. A list of bread, eggs, and milk,
wave-spray shattering over the seawall,
then blind sensations, and now, the drift
too brilliant to see, the crunch
of steps approaching.

Saturnesque

The lopsided star twirls over the horizon
and a dolphin laughs at his shadow
since the shining is so gaudy.

My mother and I stand on the balcony
high above the tropical sea
with the runway to Saturn spilling toward us.

Once again she says the sea is beautiful,
nothing induces peace like such a night.
Then she sighs unevenly and I think of a joke.

Strung and splotched with lights
the cruise ship is embraced by a sea
that shudders with love and aversion.

Under the mirthful scorn of a capering god
one must feint, one must evade,
in the manner of a darting aquatic creature.

The Disappeared were lashed to railroad ties,
then tipped into the sea from helicopters.
But this night has no mournful allure.

When El Presidente rises from bed like a parent
nothing may be hidden from him. His people don't want
to be understood, they want privacy.

My mother, as a girl, tumbled over the handlebars
into a roadside ditch, bullets ripping down the road.
Then she hoisted herself above the world.

Although sharp things flung about the galaxy
encircled in taunting bands of debris,
she could be found at night, buoyed by Jack Benny.

I think of her singing "But Beautiful,"
as if she hadn't decided to disintegrate,
as if Ella Fitzgerald had come to clean her house.

When the dark tides rose,
no one could reach her, except harshly.
How far I am from what I'd cure with words.

Yet I welcome this blithe drift away,
what's seen in a quick squint,
and the crazing, shattering path gleaming back.

Reunion

I attended the reunion,
talk brisk but diluted by time.
A colleague raised his glass
to praise me, *His legacy here is legendary.*
Not one of us knows what I was like.

News of former colleagues, vanished friends—
this one was commended, that one was broken
by onerous obligations, and she is dissatisfied
but no longer ill.

Looking down six stories, I saw a woman
approaching the office tower across the avenue,
her right arm swinging, the other slightly bent
at the elbow, in motion yet not released,
suggesting all that remains to be done.

Next time I looked out the window,
darkness had taken the city below.
There was the time in Sydney,
in Barcelona, São Paolo, and Rome.
Apparently everywhere I went
I said and did remarkable things.

Aloft, above cities, one encountered women
with no taste for nonsense. I told a lady in Amsterdam

I was an astronaut, she said you're too small,
I said this is an advantage in a capsule.

Crude forsakings of faces and cities—
the memory of my farewells
makes me sad, their wordplay,
so much charm, but not much else.
Yet I lived in a larger world. My worries,
paltry and ridiculous, disappeared in dialogue.
And then I was alone and pleasantly spent.

Of our buildings, corridors and moveable walls,
what I recall is a slender wrist and hand
reaching for a slice of toast sliding
down the exit ramp of the toaster.
The cafeteria, a place of suspensions,
surprising postures, and revelations.

I was adept at envisioning a world
of invention and speed,
then swiftly abandoning it for another,
until it seemed no great matter
to enter the world. To think
you are entering, earning, providing.

At the revolving door of the office tower
she paused—an extraordinary act,
a woman stopping cold like that—
making me a stranger to our past.

Lament

You should be here with me
during this drenching autumn.
It seems the man who delights in you
gives up the oppression of the future.
I don't care if the rain erodes my house.

The earth is squelchy
with a staining excess.
The worm and the slug,
not for a morning, not forever,
drift by in the same direction.

This year sap is plentiful but dilute.
The maples fail to produce famous colors —
leaves shrivel in a late blight
and fall, and even the falling
has lost its allure, in soaking stillness.

My affection lives in my affection,
there's no gift I want to give you,
and nothing you need in the showcases.
Such kindness would be a blunder,
like doing a favor for a deluge.

Praxis is your passion, you speak tenderly
only after exertion and exceeding,
you are accessible after completion,
so stroking you had a purpose
and pleasure, perhaps they were related.

Wild turkeys are stalking the yard,
I pretend you have sent them to me.
A rotten railing drips a bitter rebuke.
When the nuthatch leaves, the feeder sways
like the ghost of gratification.

If you were here with me,
capsules of rain would fall into the mouth
of the earth, and the rain sounding
on the windows would seduce you
into dormancy, beside me in the dark.

after Pasternak

At the Hull Gut

A 700-foot-wide rip
between the tip of Hull and Peddocks Island.
We would say, standing on the rocky beach at the point,
there are two choices, moving through or moving to.
The 590-foot tanker *Arrestado*, 35,000 tons,
the 16-foot homemade sailboat *Frolic*,
just 15 feet between them, port to port.
Propellers churning a parlous route between bay and outer harbor,
from marinas, terminals, yacht clubs, and shipyard to the open sea.
If she said "We're too intent on turning experience
into results," I'd reply "The state of one's mind
isn't an end in itself." Or if I said "When we name things,
vessels and shore life, there's an affirmation at the mind's expense,"
she'd reply "Only since the mind is so determined."
A lighthouse on the island stayed impartial,
watching sailboats sucked into the surge, out of wind.
The universal sound of peril—five bursts of a ship's horn.
And alarm swamped the beauty of our thoughts,
now dependent on mutual regard
to salvage both the plan and its fulfillment.

Final Trip

I had a Japanese colleague who drove me at four A.M.
from Tokyo along the coast to Kujukurihama Beach
to witness the advent of the Festival of the Dead.
As a gift, since this trip would be my last.

There were mounds of black volcanic sand,
holes pitting the expanse, and within each hole
a small boy curled like a shrimp.
Then the sun rose and the boys awoke,
scanning the east for the ancestral barges,
to hail the dead for a three-day visit.

The ardor of hope for the afterlife —
hearing Christians talk of it on TV
makes me uneasy. That they should be so taken.
Yet once I also counted on everlasting life.

The next week, my Italian manager sent me up
to Borgo Sansepolcro to look at *The Resurrection*
by Piero della Francesca. While four soldiers sleep,
Christ pauses, one foot up on the sarcophagus,
gazing, not at us, but through us.

In the world, I was known as a touring overseer
with a universal phone, in the habit of speaking fraternally
but actually quite formally with my local friends,
so I had to wonder why they wanted me to see these things.

Soon the boys on the beach began their walk home,
leading their invisible forebears.
The traditional festival foods of Chiba Prefecture—
dried apples, beans and chestnuts, clams,
the blowfish called *fugu*—now come from China.

A god staring through me—it's always uncertain
whether I'm about to be punished,
rewarded, or simply ignored.

Returning to my office, I packed up the few things
that didn't belong to the company.

I can't recall the names of my colleagues.
Faces drift out of the mind—
maybe that's how the afterlife arose,
first the difficulty of meeting the stranger,
and then his disappearance
into the thing he wants you to see.

Mountain Story

Those men, mornings they gather
to drink glasses of tea, play backgammon —
the Caucasus Mountains loafing all around.

Over Koran chanting from loudspeakers across the river
they repeat the tales that tell who they are.
I was looking at their photograph.

These last few years — how would I tell them my story?
I'd journeyed a ways up a mountainside,
taught the children of a sheep farmer to read and write

for food and shelter. One day he returned from the market
having exchanged a lamb for a plaster statue
of a female figure, but the drape of her robe

revealed too much, so he moved her to the woods
near my hut. The things I imagined,
it seemed like fate when she appeared at that time.

But soon I regained my customary outlook —
a woman may love but not necessarily
have a knack for affection. The children cried when I left.

In an hour I was back in town,
wondering what I'd wanted up there, why those solitary nights
seemed more intimate than a honeymoon.

Back to earning honest pay, I'm also spilling the dice,
moving my pieces on the board. While persuading you
to invest in my latest venture, I feel

her cool hand on my face.
She said to me — *If only I were not fixed in defeat,*
if only you were not determined to succeed.

The Transit of Mercury

A black dot speeding across
the solar disc—please don't
look up, just imagine it.
I offer nothing to help
you see the actual world,
but this isn't poverty,
seeing isn't what we do
in situations like this.
My personal history—
easily I made myself
invisible, I could snap
a lock soundlessly, make off
with your beagle for a day,
sing my grandfather to sleep
and pick his pocket. Thieving
isn't burglary if one's
temperament is buoyant.
Unseen, unheard—what could I
do about a finished war?
Set up my plastic men, make
them speak. One day my mother
opened her purse to find two
soldiers poised to throw grenades.
On film, façades of Europe
fell in the streets. Nurses walked
by our house between the bus

stop and the brick hospital.
Some of them acknowledged me.
And recognized among them,
I then discovered the way
to select and be chosen.
I will tell you a story
that at first will seem quite sad.
There was a god called the Spell-
binder, he of the stealthy
disposition, full of guile,
yet a patron of mankind,
whose tricks taught technical skill,
beside whose roadside pillars
strangers could risk conversing
under his protection (since
men identified themselves
by deceits they set aside),
invent mutual consent.
But then, when the Age of Kings
arrived, the god was deployed
as acolyte, a herald
of gods more ambitiously
at work in the growing world.
How I enjoyed that cigar
and martini in the famous
Ritz Bar—drunk on timelessness

in Paris, our business done.
So many smooth vintages!
The enterprising gods ruled.
Hesiod said the culture
of his era was a curse,
potter angry with potter,
carpenter with carpenter,
everyone in the market
prodded by profit. This god,
he was the one who provoked
Pandora to spill it all,
leaving only hope within—
was hope also a poison?
Or from perilous assets
did we make a vital world?
Thus this god of invention
and theft made his big comeback
while Hesiod lamented.
Designating the crossroads,
he insisted one person
could trade with an entire world.
Obviously, I feel some affinity
for his slick agility.
Professional boundary
crosser is what I became,
I stole a beautiful wife

over the line and was loved
by her father anyway,
I sold many useful objects
that soon were obsolete,
I went to the marketplace
for electric estrangements,
to dream my next attachment.
The god expedites this work,
proud sponsor of gain and loss,
and if this life is revenge
for what goes on in the mind—
still we talk here leisurely
during the five-hour transit
of Mercury, racing, then
gone for another eight years.

Fast Ferry

I am coming toward you,
speaking as I go, faster than ever.

We both know it's too late for me
to build toward an exalted ending,

all I can do now is start things.
This torn ticket, the trip you've offered

to please yourself—I'd rather create
an entire region from it, a dock teeming

with departures, thrusted jetties, shoals and spits,
than imagine what your face is forever

too reticent or oblique to tell me.
Today I'll arrange my own advantage,

a destination, a delirium
of expectation. The hazard of speed

swells the wake of escape—
but reverence of you requires a certain reserve,

a careful recovery of what survives
the dissolution of my mainland life.

I have to think of me. You've made this passage possible,
but after all, I'm just a commuter.

So this is my spillway,
already I can see workers on the wharf

taking their positions, having to hustle
now that this transit no longer takes hours.

I've decided it will be by these words,
not my silences, that I will disappear toward you,

a nearly weightless thing, speeding,
barely breaking the surface.

Now your face is fast before me,
your distaste for intrusion, the song you sing

about loneliness, and the other of solitude,
and the dread of dying unloved,

your stride among pallets, crates and rubbish,
your thoughts cast out on the waters.

Acknowledgments

To Louise Glück, my deepest gratitude for helping me weed and feed these poems and complete this book. *Voi me levate sì, ch'i' son più ch'io.*

To my editor, Michael Collier, and to Liz Lee, Larry Cooper, Michael Webb, and Melissa Lotfy, thank you for your support and efforts in publishing this book.

Many thanks to the editors of the following publications where these poems first appeared, some in earlier versions: *Blackbird:* "Reunion"; *Margie:* "Four Roses"; *Paris Review:* "The Great Wave"; *Ploughshares:* "Under the Pergola."

"At the Swedish Embassy": The lines "Every person is a half-open door / leading to a room for everyone" are quoted from the poem "The Half-Finished Heaven" by Tomas Tranströmer, translated by Robert Bly, in the collection of that title (Graywolf, 2001).

"Dinner for My Fifty-sixth Birthday": The first two lines are quoted from "A Song of a Pure-Hearted Girl" by Mêng Chiao, in *The Chinese Translations* by Witter Bynner (Farrar, Straus and Giroux, 1978).

"Beginning with a Line from Madeleine des Roches": *"Veux-tu sçavoir passant, quell a esté mon estre?"* translated by Norman R. Shapiro, in *French Women Poets of Nine Centuries* (Johns Hopkins University Press, 2008).

In "Lament," the second stanza includes an adaptation of lines by Pasternak in his poem "There Were," as translated by Mark Rudman in *My Sister—Life* (Northwestern University Press, 1983).

"Foghorn, Daybreak" is for Floyd Skloot.

"Fast Ferry" is for Anne Phaneuf.